My Tablet

NAME: _____

I will stand my watch
And set myself on the rampart,
And watch to see what He will say to me,
And what I will answer when I am corrected.
Then the Lord answered me and said: "Write
the vision
And make *it* plain on tablets,
That he may run who reads it.
Habakkuk 2:1-2 (New King James Version)

I created this guided journal by inspiration of the Holy Spirit to guide his children as they study His Word. It includes quotes or prompts that the Lord has given me during my study of His Word. It is my hope that you'll use this journal to document your visions and goals that the Lord has placed in your heart. Believing that they will surely be manifested.

Kevin Abankwa

Prayer is a communication, when you're done; listen.

Date: ___ / ___ / _____

_____
_____
_____
_____
_____
_____
_____
_____
_____
_____
_____
_____
_____
_____
_____
_____
_____
_____
_____
_____
_____
_____
_____
_____
_____
_____
_____
_____

Date: ___ / ___ / _____

_____
_____
_____
_____
_____
_____
_____
_____
_____
_____
_____
_____
_____
_____
_____
_____
_____
_____
_____
_____
_____
_____
_____
_____
_____
_____
_____
_____
_____
_____
_____

And what *is* the exceeding greatness of His power toward
us who believe, according to the working of His mighty
power
Ephesians 1:19 [NKJV]

You may never know it's possible to fly when all your friends are penguins & ostriches. Association matters!

Date: ___ / ___ / _____

_____
_____
_____
_____
_____
_____
_____
_____
_____
_____
_____
_____
_____
_____
_____
_____
_____
_____
_____
_____
_____
_____
_____
_____
_____
_____
_____

Date: ___ / ___ / _____

_____
_____
_____
_____
_____
_____
_____
_____
_____
_____
_____
_____
_____
_____
_____
_____
_____
_____
_____
_____
_____
_____
_____
_____
_____
_____
_____
_____
_____
_____

He who walks with wise *men* will be wise,
But the companion of fools will be destroyed.
Proverbs 13:20 [NKJV]

A talent (seed) well developed becomes a skill (fruit bearing tree). That skill is what translates into wealth. Remember we are trees of righteousness!

Date: ___ / ___ / _____

_____
_____
_____
_____
_____
_____
_____
_____
_____
_____
_____
_____
_____
_____
_____
_____
_____
_____
_____
_____
_____
_____
_____
_____

Date: ___ / ___ / _____

_____
_____
_____
_____
_____
_____
_____
_____
_____
_____
_____
_____
_____
_____
_____
_____
_____
_____
_____
_____
_____
_____
_____
_____
_____
_____
_____
_____

To console those who mourn in Zion,
To give them beauty for ashes,
The oil of joy for mourning,
The garment of praise for the spirit of heaviness;
That they may be called trees of righteousness,
The planting of the Lord, that He may be glorified.
Isaiah 61:3 [NKJV]

Faith comes by hearing the Word, but manifestation comes by doing the Word.

Date: ___ / ___ / _____

_____
_____
_____
_____
_____
_____
_____
_____
_____
_____
_____
_____
_____
_____
_____
_____
_____
_____
_____
_____
_____
_____
_____
_____
_____
_____

Date: ___ / ___ / _____

But be doers of the word, and not hearers only, deceiving
yourselves.
James 1:22 [NKJV]

A branch will need to grow longer to accommodate more fruits. The more it grows the more fruits are provided. The growth comes first.

Date: ___ / ___ / _____

_____
_____
_____
_____
_____
_____
_____
_____
_____
_____
_____
_____
_____
_____
_____
_____
_____
_____
_____
_____
_____
_____
_____

Date: ___ / ___ / _____

_____
_____
_____
_____
_____
_____
_____
_____
_____
_____
_____
_____
_____
_____
_____
_____
_____
_____
_____
_____
_____
_____
_____
_____
_____
_____
_____

I am the vine, you *are* the branches. He who abides in Me,
and I in him, bears much fruit; for without Me you can
do nothing.
John 15:5 [NKJV]

What is written down becomes a doorway for manifestation.

Date: ___ / ___ / _____

Date: ___ / ___ / ____

_____
_____
_____
_____
_____
_____
_____
_____
_____
_____
_____
_____
_____
_____
_____
_____
_____
_____
_____
_____
_____
_____
_____
_____
_____
_____
_____
_____
_____
_____

Write the vision
And make *it* plain on tablets,
That he may run who reads it.
Habakkuk 2:2 [NKJV]

It's called a miracle because it's prompted or caused and acted on by faith.

Date: ___ / ___ / _____

_____
_____
_____
_____
_____
_____
_____
_____
_____
_____
_____
_____
_____
_____
_____
_____
_____
_____
_____
_____
_____
_____
_____
_____
_____
_____
_____
_____
_____
_____

Date: ___ / ___ / _____

Then He arose and rebuked the wind, and said to the
sea, "Peace, be still!" And the wind ceased and there was a
great calm.
Mark 4:39 [NKJV]

The absence of total & complete knowledge of Jesus Christ is fear. For fear is the absence of knowledge.

Date: ___ / ___ / _____

_____
_____
_____
_____
_____
_____
_____
_____
_____
_____
_____
_____
_____
_____
_____
_____
_____
_____
_____
_____
_____
_____
_____
_____
_____
_____

Date: ___ / ___ / _____

_____
_____
_____
_____
_____
_____
_____
_____
_____
_____
_____
_____
_____
_____
_____
_____
_____
_____
_____
_____
_____
_____
_____
_____
_____
_____
_____
_____
_____
_____

In whom are hidden all the treasures of wisdom and
knowledge.
Colossians 2:3 [NKJV]

The seed you place in time produces fruits in due time.

Date: ___ / ___ / _____

_____
_____
_____
_____
_____
_____
_____
_____
_____
_____
_____
_____
_____
_____
_____
_____
_____
_____
_____
_____
_____
_____
_____
_____
_____
_____
_____
_____

Date: ___ / ___ / _____

_____
_____
_____
_____
_____
_____
_____
_____
_____
_____
_____
_____
_____
_____
_____
_____
_____
_____
_____
_____
_____
_____
_____
_____
_____
_____
_____
_____
_____
_____

It is the Spirit who gives life; the flesh profits nothing.
The words that I speak to you are spirit, and *they* are life.
John 6:63 [NKJV]

His grace is always attached to an assignment.

Date: ___ / ___ / _____

_____
_____
_____
_____
_____
_____
_____
_____
_____
_____
_____
_____
_____
_____
_____
_____
_____
_____
_____
_____
_____
_____
_____
_____
_____
_____

Date: ___ / ___ / _____

_____
_____
_____
_____
_____
_____
_____
_____
_____
_____
_____
_____
_____
_____
_____
_____
_____
_____
_____
_____
_____
_____
_____
_____
_____
_____
_____
_____

To me, who am less than the least of all the saints, this
grace was given, that I should preach among the Gentiles
the unsearchable riches of Christ.
Ephesians 3:8 [NKJV]

There is no harvest without sowing. If you don't like your harvest, investigate your seed and ground.

Date: ___ / ___ / _____

_____
_____
_____
_____
_____
_____
_____
_____
_____
_____
_____
_____
_____
_____
_____
_____
_____
_____
_____
_____
_____
_____
_____
_____
_____
_____
_____

Date: ___ / ___ / _____

You cannot count the number of fruits in a seed, but you can count the number of seeds in a fruit.

Date: ___ / ___ / _____

Date: ___ / ___ / ____

_____
_____
_____
_____
_____
_____
_____
_____
_____
_____
_____
_____
_____
_____
_____
_____
_____
_____
_____
_____
_____
_____
_____
_____
_____
_____
_____
_____

So Jesus said to them, "Because of your unbelief; for
assuredly, I say to you, if you have faith as a mustard
seed, you will say to this mountain, 'Move from here to
there,' and it will move; and nothing will be impossible for
you.
Matthew 17:20 [NKJV]

Success is what you attract because of your investments.

Date: ___ / ___ / _____

_____

_____

_____

_____

_____

_____

_____

_____

_____

_____

_____

_____

_____

_____

_____

_____

_____

_____

_____

_____

_____

_____

_____

_____

_____

Date: ___ / ___ / _____

_____
_____
_____
_____
_____
_____
_____
_____
_____
_____
_____
_____
_____
_____
_____
_____
_____
_____
_____
_____
_____
_____
_____
_____
_____
_____
_____
_____
_____

This Book of the Law shall not depart from your mouth,
but you shall meditate in it day and night, that you may
observe to do according to all that is written in it. For then
you will make your way prosperous, and then you will have
good success.
Joshua 1:8 [NKJV]

The path you know as a child of God is not the only path, but the path that is specifically revealed to you to walk in.

Date: ___ / ___ / _____

_____
_____
_____
_____
_____
_____
_____
_____
_____
_____
_____
_____
_____
_____
_____
_____
_____
_____
_____
_____
_____
_____
_____
_____
_____
_____
_____
_____

Date: ___ / ___ / _____

However, when He, the Spirit of truth, has come, He will
guide you into all truth; for He will not speak on His
own *authority*, but whatever He hears He will speak; and
He will tell you things to come.
John 16:13 [NKJV]   **28**

Pray with your mouth, also pray with your heart.

Date: ___ / ___ / _____

_____
_____
_____
_____
_____
_____
_____
_____
_____
_____
_____
_____
_____
_____
_____
_____
_____
_____
_____
_____
_____
_____
_____
_____
_____
_____
_____

Date: ___ / ___ / ___

_____
_____
_____
_____
_____
_____
_____
_____
_____
_____
_____
_____
_____
_____
_____
_____
_____
_____
_____
_____
_____
_____
_____
_____
_____
_____
_____
_____
_____

These people draw near to Me with their mouth,
And honor Me with *their* lips,
But their heart is far from Me.
Matthew 15:8 [NKJV]

Anything that is of high value is hidden. It is your steadfast pursuit that reveals it.

Date: ___ / ___ / _____

_____
_____
_____
_____
_____
_____
_____
_____
_____
_____
_____
_____
_____
_____
_____
_____
_____
_____
_____
_____
_____
_____
_____
_____

Date: ___ / ___ / ____

_____
_____
_____
_____
_____
_____
_____
_____
_____
_____
_____
_____
_____
_____
_____
_____
_____
_____
_____
_____
_____
_____
_____
_____
_____
_____
_____
_____
_____
_____
_____
_____

And you will seek Me and find *Me,* when you search for
Me with all your heart.
Jeremiah 29:13 [NKJV]

*Remember when God opens a door,
sometimes satan opens a gate to distract &
destroy.*

Date: ___ / ___ / _____

_____
_____
_____
_____
_____
_____
_____
_____
_____
_____
_____
_____
_____
_____
_____
_____
_____
_____
_____
_____
_____
_____
_____
_____

Date: ___ / ___ / _____

_____
_____
_____
_____
_____
_____
_____
_____
_____
_____
_____
_____
_____
_____
_____
_____
_____
_____
_____
_____
_____
_____
_____
_____
_____
_____
_____
_____

Your ears shall hear a word behind you, saying,
"This *is* the way, walk in it," whenever you turn to the right
hand or whenever you turn to the left.
Isaiah 30:21 [NKJV]

Uncomfortable Truth: Only situations can prove the heart of a person.

Date: ___ / ___ / _____

_____
_____
_____
_____
_____
_____
_____
_____
_____
_____
_____
_____
_____
_____
_____
_____
_____
_____
_____
_____
_____
_____
_____
_____
_____
_____
_____
_____

Date: ___ / ___ / _____

_____
_____
_____
_____
_____
_____
_____
_____
_____
_____
_____
_____
_____
_____
_____
_____
_____
_____
_____
_____
_____
_____
_____
_____
_____
_____
_____
_____
_____
_____

He who says he abides in Him ought himself also to walk
just as He walked.
1 John 2:6 [NKJV]

Training may not always be pleasant, but it's needed for your inheritance.

Date: ___ / ___ / _____

_____
_____
_____
_____
_____
_____
_____
_____
_____
_____
_____
_____
_____
_____
_____
_____
_____
_____
_____
_____
_____
_____
_____
_____
_____
_____
_____

Date: ___ / ___ / _____

_____
_____
_____
_____
_____
_____
_____
_____
_____
_____
_____
_____
_____
_____
_____
_____
_____
_____
_____
_____
_____
_____
_____
_____
_____
_____
_____
_____
_____
_____

He teaches my hands to make war,
So that my arms can bend a bow of bronze.
Psalm 18:34 [NKJV]

Success is what you've done compared to what you were created to do at the appointed time.

Date: ___ / ___ / _____

_____
_____
_____
_____
_____
_____
_____
_____
_____
_____
_____
_____
_____
_____
_____
_____
_____
_____
_____
_____
_____
_____
_____
_____

Date: ___ / ___ / _____

_____
_____
_____
_____
_____
_____
_____
_____
_____
_____
_____
_____
_____
_____
_____
_____
_____
_____
_____
_____
_____
_____
_____
_____
_____
_____
_____
_____

He who sins is of the devil, for the devil has sinned from
the beginning. For this purpose the Son of God was
manifested, that He might destroy the works of the devil.
1 John 3:8 [NKJV]

Working hard and praying fervently brings divinity into humanity.

Date: ___ / ___ / _____

_____

_____

_____

_____

_____

_____

_____

_____

_____

_____

_____

_____

_____

_____

_____

_____

_____

_____

_____

_____

_____

_____

_____

_____

_____

_____

_____

_____

_____

Date: ___ / ___ / ____

_____
_____
_____
_____
_____
_____
_____
_____
_____
_____
_____
_____
_____
_____
_____
_____
_____
_____
_____
_____
_____
_____
_____
_____
_____
_____
_____
_____
_____
_____
_____

And whatever you do, do it heartily, as to the Lord and not
to men
Colossians 3:23 [NKJV]

Do not exchange your reward from God for an award from men.

Date: ___ / ___ / _____

_____
_____
_____
_____
_____
_____
_____
_____
_____
_____
_____
_____
_____
_____
_____
_____
_____
_____
_____
_____
_____
_____
_____
_____
_____
_____
_____

Date: ___ / ___ / ____

_____
_____
_____
_____
_____
_____
_____
_____
_____
_____
_____
_____
_____
_____
_____
_____
_____
_____
_____
_____
_____
_____
_____
_____
_____
_____
_____
_____
_____
_____
_____

Take heed that you do not do your charitable deeds before
men, to be seen by them. Otherwise you have no reward
from your Father in heaven.
Matthew 6:1 [NKJV]

Your orthopraxy shows your orthodoxy.

Date: ___ / ___ / _____

_____

_____

_____

_____

_____

_____

_____

_____

_____

_____

_____

_____

_____

_____

_____

_____

_____

_____

_____

_____

_____

_____

_____

_____

_____

_____

_____

Date: ___ / ___ / _____

I know that you are Abraham's descendants, but you seek
to kill Me, because My word has no place in you.
John 8:37 [NKJV]

Make sure what you know doesn't become a stumbling block to what you need to know.

Date: ___ / ___ / _____

_____
_____
_____
_____
_____
_____
_____
_____
_____
_____
_____
_____
_____
_____
_____
_____
_____
_____
_____
_____
_____
_____
_____
_____
_____

Date: ___ / ___ / _____

_____
_____
_____
_____
_____
_____
_____
_____
_____
_____
_____
_____
_____
_____
_____
_____
_____
_____
_____
_____
_____
_____
_____
_____
_____
_____
_____
_____
_____

But Peter said, "Not so, Lord! For I have never eaten
anything common or unclean." And a voice *spoke* to him
again the second time, "What God has cleansed you must
not call common."
Acts 10:14-15 [NKJV]

Your character is a door, make sure you're always holding the key.

Date: ___ / ___ / _____

_____
_____
_____
_____
_____
_____
_____
_____
_____
_____
_____
_____
_____
_____
_____
_____
_____
_____
_____
_____
_____
_____
_____
_____
_____
_____
_____

Date: ___ / ___ / _____

_____
_____
_____
_____
_____
_____
_____
_____
_____
_____
_____
_____
_____
_____
_____
_____
_____
_____
_____
_____
_____
_____
_____
_____
_____
_____
_____
_____

That the genuineness of your faith, *being* much more
precious than gold that perishes, though it is tested by
fire, may be found to praise, honor, and glory at the
revelation of Jesus Christ
1 Peter 1:7 [NKJV]

Understanding of God's Word brings faith,
faith tested reveals your trust in Him.

Date: ___ / ___ / _____

_____
_____
_____
_____
_____
_____
_____
_____
_____
_____
_____
_____
_____
_____
_____
_____
_____
_____
_____
_____
_____
_____
_____
_____
_____
_____
_____
_____
_____

Date: ___ / ___ / _____

_____
_____
_____
_____
_____
_____
_____
_____
_____
_____
_____
_____
_____
_____
_____
_____
_____
_____
_____
_____
_____
_____
_____
_____
_____
_____
_____
_____
_____

That the genuineness of your faith, *being* much more
precious than gold that perishes, though it is tested by
fire, may be found to praise, honor, and glory at the
revelation of Jesus Christ
1 Peter 1:7 [NKJV]

The knowledge of the Word of God is the transportation for your inheritance.

Date: ___ / ___ / _____

_____
_____
_____
_____
_____
_____
_____
_____
_____
_____
_____
_____
_____
_____
_____
_____
_____
_____
_____
_____
_____
_____
_____
_____

Date: ___ / ___ / _____

_____
_____
_____
_____
_____
_____
_____
_____
_____
_____
_____
_____
_____
_____
_____
_____
_____
_____
_____
_____
_____
_____
_____
_____
_____
_____
_____
_____
_____

So now, brethren, I commend you to God and to the word
of His grace, which is able to build you up and give you an
inheritance among all those who are sanctified.
Acts 20:32 [NKJV]

The knowledge of God is the continuous revelation of application of the truths in God's Word.

Date: ___ / ___ / _____

_____
_____
_____
_____
_____
_____
_____
_____
_____
_____
_____
_____
_____
_____
_____
_____
_____
_____
_____
_____
_____
_____
_____
_____

Date: ___ / ___ / _____

_____
_____
_____
_____
_____
_____
_____
_____
_____
_____
_____
_____
_____
_____
_____
_____
_____
_____
_____
_____
_____
_____
_____
_____
_____
_____
_____
_____
_____
_____
_____

For this reason I will not be negligent to remind you always
of these things, though you know and are established in
the present truth.
2 Peter 1:12 [NKJV]

*Appealing leaves but no fruits. Let your
fruits define you, not your leaves.*

Date: ___ / ___ / _____

Date: ___ / ___ / _____

_____
_____
_____
_____
_____
_____
_____
_____
_____
_____
_____
_____
_____
_____
_____
_____
_____
_____
_____
_____
_____
_____
_____
_____
_____
_____
_____
_____
_____
_____
_____

Let your light so shine before men, that they may see your
good works and glorify your Father in heaven.
Matthew 5:16 [NKJV]

Miracles causes believe but for a moment, but the Word of God establishes your beliefs.

Date: ___ / ___ / _____

_____
_____
_____
_____
_____
_____
_____
_____
_____
_____
_____
_____
_____
_____
_____
_____
_____
_____
_____
_____
_____
_____
_____
_____
_____
_____

Date: ___ / ___ / _____

_____
_____
_____
_____
_____
_____
_____
_____
_____
_____
_____
_____
_____
_____
_____
_____
_____
_____
_____
_____
_____
_____
_____
_____
_____
_____
_____
_____

Now we have received, not the spirit of the world, but the
Spirit who is from God, that we might know the things that
have been freely given to us by God.
1 Corinthians 2:12 [NKJV]

Your root determines your fruitfulness.

Date: ___ / ___ / _____

_____

_____

_____

_____

_____

_____

_____

_____

_____

_____

_____

_____

_____

_____

_____

_____

_____

_____

_____

_____

_____

_____

_____

_____

_____

_____

_____

_____

Date: ___ / ___ / _____

_____
_____
_____
_____
_____
_____
_____
_____
_____
_____
_____
_____
_____
_____
_____
_____
_____
_____
_____
_____
_____
_____
_____
_____
_____
_____

That Christ may dwell in your hearts through faith; that
you, being rooted and grounded in love, may be able to
comprehend with all the saints what *is* the width and length
and depth and height— to know the love of Christ which
passes knowledge; that you may be filled with all the
fullness of God.
Ephesians 3:17-19 [NKJV]

You cannot forget what you've kept in your Spirit.

Date: ___ / ___ / _____

_____
_____
_____
_____
_____
_____
_____
_____
_____
_____
_____
_____
_____
_____
_____
_____
_____
_____
_____
_____
_____
_____
_____
_____
_____
_____
_____
_____

Date: ___ / ___ / ____

But the Helper, the Holy Spirit, whom the Father will send
in My name, He will teach you all things, and bring to
your remembrance all things that I said to you.
John 14:26 [NKJV]

The carefully planned, timely dissemination of knowledge is needed in order to maintain negentropy.

Date: ___ / ___ / _____

Date: ___ / ___ / _____

_____
_____
_____
_____
_____
_____
_____
_____
_____
_____
_____
_____
_____
_____
_____
_____
_____
_____
_____
_____
_____
_____
_____
_____
_____
_____
_____
_____

Then He commanded His disciples that they should tell no
one that He was Jesus the Christ.
Matthew 16:20 [NKJV]

Faith comes by hearing, for the Word of God brings knowledge of Him.

Date: ___ / ___ / _____

_____
_____
_____
_____
_____
_____
_____
_____
_____
_____
_____
_____
_____
_____
_____
_____
_____
_____
_____
_____
_____
_____
_____
_____
_____
_____

Date: ___ / ___ / ____

_____

_____

_____

_____

_____

_____

_____

_____

_____

_____

_____

_____

_____

_____

_____

_____

_____

_____

_____

_____

_____

_____

_____

_____

_____

_____

_____

_____

So then faith *comes* by hearing, and hearing by the word
of God.
Romans 10:17 [NKJV]

68

The more I learn, the more I know; the more I know, the more I know I do not know and I learn some more.

Date: ___ / ___ / _____

_____
_____
_____
_____
_____
_____
_____
_____
_____
_____
_____
_____
_____
_____
_____
_____
_____
_____
_____
_____
_____
_____
_____
_____
_____

Date: ___ / ___ / _____

_____
_____
_____
_____
_____
_____
_____
_____
_____
_____
_____
_____
_____
_____
_____
_____
_____
_____
_____
_____
_____
_____
_____
_____
_____
_____
_____
_____
_____

But God has revealed *them* to us through His Spirit. For
the Spirit searches all things, yes, the deep things of God.
1 Corinthians 2:10 [NKJV]

An unwavering spirit to the word of God is a growing spirit because they're rooted & grounded.

Date: ___ / ___ / _____

_____
_____
_____
_____
_____
_____
_____
_____
_____
_____
_____
_____
_____
_____
_____
_____
_____
_____
_____
_____
_____
_____
_____
_____
_____

Date: ___ / ___ / _____

_____
_____
_____
_____
_____
_____
_____
_____
_____
_____
_____
_____
_____
_____
_____
_____
_____
_____
_____
_____
_____
_____
_____
_____
_____
_____
_____
_____
_____
_____
_____

But whoever keeps His word, truly the love of God is
perfected in him. By this we know that we are in Him.
1 John 2:5 [NKJV]

You can never outgrow the need for divine direction.

Date: ___ / ___ / _____

_____
_____
_____
_____
_____
_____
_____
_____
_____
_____
_____
_____
_____
_____
_____
_____
_____
_____
_____
_____
_____
_____
_____
_____
_____
_____
_____

Date: ___ / ___ / ____

However, when He, the Spirit of truth, has come, He will
guide you into all truth; for He will not speak on His
own *authority,* but whatever He hears He will speak; and
He will tell you things to come.
John 16:13 [NKJV]

Advancing from one class to another comes after passing a test. Until the test is passed, there is no advancement.

Date: ___ / ___ / _____

_____
_____
_____
_____
_____
_____
_____
_____
_____
_____
_____
_____
_____
_____
_____
_____
_____
_____
_____
_____
_____
_____
_____
_____
_____
_____

Date: ___ / ___ / _____

_____
_____
_____
_____
_____
_____
_____
_____
_____
_____
_____
_____
_____
_____
_____
_____
_____
_____
_____
_____
_____
_____
_____
_____
_____
_____
_____
_____
_____
_____

If anyone's work which he has built on *it* endures, he will
receive a reward. If anyone's work is burned, he will suffer
loss; but he himself will be saved, yet so as through fire.
1 Corinthians 3:14-15 [NKJV]

The accurate & precise knowledge of God's Word is like jet fuel, the more you have the longer your distance of travel.

Date: ___ / ___ / _____

_____
_____
_____
_____
_____
_____
_____
_____
_____
_____
_____
_____
_____
_____
_____
_____
_____
_____
_____
_____
_____
_____
_____
_____
_____
_____
_____

Date: ___ / ___ / _____

_____

_____

_____

_____

_____

_____

_____

_____

_____

_____

_____

_____

_____

_____

_____

_____

_____

_____

_____

_____

_____

_____

_____

_____

_____

_____

My son, give attention to my words; Incline your ear to my
sayings. Do not let them depart from your eyes; Keep them
in the midst of your heart; For they *are* life to those who
find them, And health to all their flesh.
Proverbs 4:20-22 [NKJV]

Believing is the water that waters the seed of words that are implanted in our spirit.

Date: ___ / ___ / _____

_____
_____
_____
_____
_____
_____
_____
_____
_____
_____
_____
_____
_____
_____
_____
_____
_____
_____
_____
_____
_____
_____
_____
_____
_____
_____
_____
_____
_____

Date: ___ / ___ / ____

_____
_____
_____
_____
_____
_____
_____
_____
_____
_____
_____
_____
_____
_____
_____
_____
_____
_____
_____
_____
_____
_____
_____
_____
_____
_____
_____
_____

Jesus said to him, "If you can believe, all
things *are* possible to him who believes."
Mark 9:23 [NKJV]

Preaching is for hearers, and teaching is for learners.

Date: ___ / ___ / _____

_____
_____
_____
_____
_____
_____
_____
_____
_____
_____
_____
_____
_____
_____
_____
_____
_____
_____
_____
_____
_____
_____
_____
_____
_____
_____
_____
_____

Date: ___ / ___ / _____

_____
_____
_____
_____
_____
_____
_____
_____
_____
_____
_____
_____
_____
_____
_____
_____
_____
_____
_____
_____
_____
_____
_____
_____
_____
_____

And Jesus went about all Galilee, teaching in their
synagogues, preaching the gospel of the kingdom, and
healing all kinds of sickness and all kinds of disease among
the people.
Matthew 4:23 [NKJV]

Revelation precedes manifestation. The light first then life.

Date: ___ / ___ / _____

_____
_____
_____
_____
_____
_____
_____
_____
_____
_____
_____
_____
_____
_____
_____
_____
_____
_____
_____
_____
_____
_____
_____
_____
_____
_____
_____

Date: ___ / ___ / _____

_____
_____
_____
_____
_____
_____
_____
_____
_____
_____
_____
_____
_____
_____
_____
_____
_____
_____
_____
_____
_____
_____
_____
_____
_____
_____
_____

And in a vision he has seen a man named Ananias coming
in and putting *his* hand on him, so that he might receive his
sight.
Acts 9:12 [NKJV]

*Your heartily expression in worship shows
your value of His communion.*

Date: ___ / ___ / _____

_____
_____
_____
_____
_____
_____
_____
_____
_____
_____
_____
_____
_____
_____
_____
_____
_____
_____
_____
_____
_____
_____
_____
_____
_____

For Solomon had made a bronze platform five cubits long,
five cubits wide, and three cubits high, and had set it in the
midst of the court; and he stood on it, knelt down on his
knees before all the assembly of Israel, and spread out his
hands toward heaven
2 Chronicles 6:13 [NKJV]

Those who initiate & pursue peace are the peacemakers.

Date: ___ / ___ / _____

_____
_____
_____
_____
_____
_____
_____
_____
_____
_____
_____
_____
_____
_____
_____
_____
_____
_____
_____
_____
_____
_____
_____
_____
_____
_____

Date: ___ / ___ / _____

_____
_____
_____
_____
_____
_____
_____
_____
_____
_____
_____
_____
_____
_____
_____
_____
_____
_____
_____
_____
_____
_____
_____
_____
_____
_____
_____

Blessed *are* the peacemakers,
For they shall be called sons of God.
Matthew 5:9 [NKJV]

Don't be like those whose prayers are like praying against gravity. Forgetting that it was created by the Word of God.

Date: ___ / ___ / _____

_____
_____
_____
_____
_____
_____
_____
_____
_____
_____
_____
_____
_____
_____
_____
_____
_____
_____
_____
_____
_____
_____
_____
_____
_____

Date: ___ / ___ / _____

_____

_____

_____

_____

_____

_____

_____

_____

_____

_____

_____

_____

_____

_____

_____

_____

_____

_____

_____

_____

_____

_____

_____

_____

_____

_____

The Lord by wisdom founded the earth;
By understanding He established the heavens
Proverbs 3:19 [NKJV]

Authority & Power is demonstrated and confirmed by works.

Date: ___ / ___ / _____

Date: ___ / ___ / ____

_____
_____
_____
_____
_____
_____
_____
_____
_____
_____
_____
_____
_____
_____
_____
_____
_____
_____
_____
_____
_____
_____
_____
_____
_____
_____
_____
_____
_____

And they went out and preached everywhere, the Lord
working with *them* and confirming the word through the
accompanying signs. Amen.
Mark 16:20 [NKJV]

The world may say "wait and see" but we say "watch and pray".

Date: ___ / ___ / _____

Date: ___ / ___ / _____

Watch and pray, lest you enter into temptation. The spirit
indeed *is* willing, but the flesh *is* weak.
Matthew 26:41 [NKJV]

To preach means to declare, to teach means to explain. Preaching gives you knowledge, teaching gives you understanding.

Date: ___ / ___ / _____

_____
_____
_____
_____
_____
_____
_____
_____
_____
_____
_____
_____
_____
_____
_____
_____
_____
_____
_____
_____
_____
_____
_____
_____
_____

Date: ___ / ___ / _____

Then He went down to Capernaum, a city of Galilee, and
was teaching them on the Sabbaths. And they
were astonished at His teaching, for His word was with
authority.
Luke 4:31-32 [NKJV]

The kingdom of God is preached, the Word of God is thought.

Date: ___ / ___ / _____

_____
_____
_____
_____
_____
_____
_____
_____
_____
_____
_____
_____
_____
_____
_____
_____
_____
_____
_____
_____
_____
_____
_____
_____
_____
_____
_____
_____

Date: ___ / ___ / ____

_____
_____
_____
_____
_____
_____
_____
_____
_____
_____
_____
_____
_____
_____
_____
_____
_____
_____
_____
_____
_____
_____
_____
_____
_____
_____
_____
_____

And Jesus went about all Galilee, teaching in their
synagogues, preaching the gospel of the kingdom, and
healing all kinds of sickness and all kinds of disease among
the people.
Matthew 4:23 [NKJV]

Grace not explained is grace abused.

Date: ___ / ___ / _____

Date: ___ / ___ / ____

_____
_____
_____
_____
_____
_____
_____
_____
_____
_____
_____
_____
_____
_____
_____
_____
_____
_____
_____
_____
_____
_____
_____
_____
_____
_____

What shall we say then? Shall we continue in sin, that
grace may abound? God forbid. How shall we, that are dead
to sin, live any longer therein?
Romans 6:1-2 [NKJV]

Information brings knowledge, knowledge brings illumination, illumination brings revelations, and revelations bring vision.

Date: ___ / ___ / _____

_____
_____
_____
_____
_____
_____
_____
_____
_____
_____
_____
_____
_____
_____
_____
_____
_____
_____
_____
_____
_____
_____
_____
_____

Date: ___ / ___ / ____

_____
_____
_____
_____
_____
_____
_____
_____
_____
_____
_____
_____
_____
_____
_____
_____
_____
_____
_____
_____
_____
_____
_____
_____
_____
_____
_____
_____

For this *is* good and acceptable in the sight of God our
Savior, who desires all men to be saved and to come to the
knowledge of the truth.
1 Timothy 2:3-4 [NKJV]

Don't ask for rain when there is no seed in the ground.

Date: ___ / ___ / _____

_____
_____
_____
_____
_____
_____
_____
_____
_____
_____
_____
_____
_____
_____
_____
_____
_____
_____
_____
_____
_____
_____
_____
_____
_____
_____

Date: ___ / ___ / _____

_____
_____
_____
_____
_____
_____
_____
_____
_____
_____
_____
_____
_____
_____
_____
_____
_____
_____
_____
_____
_____
_____
_____
_____
_____
_____
_____
_____
_____
_____

"While the earth remains, Seedtime and harvest,
Cold and heat, Winter and summer, And day and night
Shall not cease."
Genesis 8:22 [NKJV]

The absence of the total and complete knowledge of Jesus is fear.

Date: ___ / ___ / _____

Date: ___ / ___ / ____

_____
_____
_____
_____
_____
_____
_____
_____
_____
_____
_____
_____
_____
_____
_____
_____
_____
_____
_____
_____
_____
_____
_____
_____
_____
_____
_____

There is no fear in love; but perfect love casts out fear,
because fear involves torment. But he who fears has not
been made perfect in love.
1 John 4:18 [NKJV]

Value is in purpose, find your purpose and discover your value.

Date: ___ / ___ / _____

_____
_____
_____
_____
_____
_____
_____
_____
_____
_____
_____
_____
_____
_____
_____
_____
_____
_____
_____
_____
_____
_____
_____
_____
_____

Date: ___ / ___ / ____

_____
_____
_____
_____
_____
_____
_____
_____
_____
_____
_____
_____
_____
_____
_____
_____
_____
_____
_____
_____
_____
_____
_____
_____
_____
_____
_____
_____
_____
_____
_____

You are the salt of the earth; but if the salt loses its flavor,
how shall it be seasoned? It is then good for nothing but to
be thrown out and trampled underfoot by men.
Matthew 5:13 [NKJV]

Knowledge is the catalyst for conviction. And conviction is the shell that carries your believe. How strong is your shell?

Date: ___ / ___ / _____

_____

_____

_____

_____

_____

_____

_____

_____

_____

_____

_____

_____

_____

_____

_____

_____

_____

_____

_____

_____

_____

_____

Date: ___ / ___ / _____

_____
_____
_____
_____
_____
_____
_____
_____
_____
_____
_____
_____
_____
_____
_____
_____
_____
_____
_____
_____
_____
_____
_____
_____
_____
_____
_____
_____

And we know that all things work together for good to
those who love God, to those who are the called according
to *His* purpose.
Romans 8:28 [NKJV]

A person's revelation is subject to his knowledge of God's Word.

Date: ___ / ___ / _____

Date: ___ / ___ / _____

_____
_____
_____
_____
_____
_____
_____
_____
_____
_____
_____
_____
_____
_____
_____
_____
_____
_____
_____
_____
_____
_____
_____
_____
_____
_____
_____
_____
_____
_____
_____
_____
_____

And Jesus increased in wisdom and stature, and in favor
with God and men.
Luke 2:52 [NKJV]

You must know his will in order to know your inheritance.

Date: ___ / ___ / _____

_____
_____
_____
_____
_____
_____
_____
_____
_____
_____
_____
_____
_____
_____
_____
_____
_____
_____
_____
_____
_____
_____
_____
_____
_____
_____
_____
_____

Date: ___ / ___ / _____

_____
_____
_____
_____
_____
_____
_____
_____
_____
_____
_____
_____
_____
_____
_____
_____
_____
_____
_____
_____
_____
_____
_____
_____
_____
_____
_____
_____

And has made us kings and priests to His God and
Father, to Him *be* glory and dominion forever and ever.
Amen.
Revelations 1:6 [NKJV]

Honor is always preceded by humility.

Date: ___ / ___ / _____

_____

_____

_____

_____

_____

_____

_____

_____

_____

_____

_____

_____

_____

_____

_____

_____

_____

_____

_____

_____

_____

_____

_____

_____

_____

_____

_____

_____

_____

_____

_____

Date: ___ / ___ / ____

The fear of the Lord *is* the instruction of wisdom,
And before honor *is* humility.
Proverbs 15:33 [NKJV]

As a mirror displays your image, so does
your image defines your identity.

Date: ___ / ___ / _____

Date: ___ / ___ / ____

_____
_____
_____
_____
_____
_____
_____
_____
_____
_____
_____
_____
_____
_____
_____
_____
_____
_____
_____
_____
_____
_____
_____
_____
_____
_____
_____
_____
_____
_____
_____
_____

But we all, with unveiled face, beholding as in a mirror the
glory of the Lord, are being transformed into the same
image from glory to glory, just as by the Spirit of the Lord.
2 Corinthians 3:18 [NKJV]

The knowledge of the word of God is not wrapped up in a gift.

Date: ___ / ___ / _____

_____
_____
_____
_____
_____
_____
_____
_____
_____
_____
_____
_____
_____
_____
_____
_____
_____
_____
_____
_____
_____
_____
_____
_____
_____
_____

Date: ___ / ___ / _____

_____
_____
_____
_____
_____
_____
_____
_____
_____
_____
_____
_____
_____
_____
_____
_____
_____
_____
_____
_____
_____
_____
_____
_____
_____
_____
_____
_____

Meditate on these things; give yourself entirely to them,
that your progress may be evident to all. Take heed to
yourself and to the doctrine. Continue in them, for in doing
this you will save both yourself and those who hear you.
1 Timothy 4:15-16 [NKJV]

We hear to understand, we see to perceive.

Date: ___ / ___ / _____

Date: ___ / ___ / ____

And He said, Go, and tell this people:
'Keep on hearing, but do not understand;
Keep on seeing, but do not perceive.'
Isaiah 6:9 [NKJV]

Date: ___ / ___ / _____

Date: ___ / ___ / _____

Date: ___ / ___ / _____

Date: ___ / ___ / ____

Date: ___ / ___ / _____

Date: ___ / ___ / ____

Date: ___ / ___ / _____

INDEX

Page

1. _____
2. _____
3. _____
4. _____
5. _____
6. _____
7. _____
8. _____
9. _____
10. _____
11. _____
12. _____
13. _____
14. _____
15. _____
16. _____
17. _____
18. _____
19. _____
20. _____
21. _____
22. _____
23. _____
24. _____
25. _____
26. _____
27. _____
28. _____

29. _____
30. _____
31. _____
32. _____
33. _____
34. _____
35. _____
36. _____
37. _____
38. _____
39. _____
40. _____
41. _____
42. _____
43. _____
44. _____
45. _____
46. _____
47. _____
48. _____
49. _____
50. _____
51. _____
52. _____
53. _____
54. _____
55. _____
56. _____
57. _____
58. _____
59. _____

60.

61.

62.

63.

64.

65.

66.

67.

68.

69.

70.

71.

72.

73.

74.

75.

76.

77.

78.

79.

80.

81.

82.

83.

84.

85.

86.

87.

88.

89.

90.

91. _____
92. _____
93. _____
94. _____
95. _____
96. _____
97. _____
98. _____
99. _____
100. _____
101. _____
102. _____
103. _____
104. _____
105. _____
106. _____
107. _____
108. _____
109. _____
110. _____
111. _____
112. _____
113. _____
114. _____
115. _____
116. _____
117. _____
118. _____
119. _____
120. _____
121. _____

122. _____

123. _____

124. _____

125. _____

126. _____

127. _____

128. _____

129. _____

130. _____

ABOUT THE AUTHOR

Kevin Abankwa is passionate for the knowledge of God's Word. Born in Accra, Ghana he loved the Lord from a young age and his knowledge of God's Word has only grown over the years. Through this journal he shares some of the thoughts the Spirit of God gives him as he studies the Word of God. Kevin is also a chemical Engineer, entrepreneur and currently pursuing his doctorate degree at Grand Canyon University. He lives in North Carolina, USA with his wife and three children.

www.ingramcontent.com/pod-product-compliance
Lightning Source LLC
Chambersburg PA
CBHW031932090426
42811CB00002B/158